Beyond the Checkout

Exploring the Future of Online Shopping

Shahid Gill

Copyright © 2023 Shahid Gill

All rights reserved.

DISCLAIMER

The information contained, included, or mentioned in this book is for general informational purposes only. The author does not provide any medical, legal, or financial advice. The author is not a medical professional, lawyer, or financial advisor. The information in this book should not be used as a substitute for professional advice. The author disclaims any liability for any loss or damage arising from the use of this information.

The author reserves the right to change or update the information in this book at any time without notice.

The author does not endorse or recommend any of the products or services mentioned in this book.

The author is not affiliated with any of the organizations or businesses mentioned in this book.

This book is for educational and entertainment purposes only.

Contents

Introduction 4

1- The Rise of Online Shopping: A Brief History 6
2- Current State of Online Shopping: Trends and Statistics 9
3- The Power of Personalization: Tailoring the Shopping Experience 12
4- Augmented Reality (AR) and Virtual Reality (VR): Transforming the Shopping Experience 15
5- Voice Commerce: From Voice Assistants to Voice-Activated Shopping 18
6- Artificial Intelligence (AI) in E-Commerce: Enhancing Recommendations and Customer Service 21
7- Mobile Commerce (M-Commerce): The Future in the Palm of Your Hand 25
8- Social Commerce: The Intersection of Social Media and Online Shopping 29
9- The Role of Blockchain in E-Commerce: Security and Transparency 33
10- Sustainability and Ethical Shopping: Navigating the Green Consumer Revolution 37
11- Omni-Channel Retailing: Seamlessly Integrating Offline and Online Shopping 41
12- The Future of Delivery: Drone, Autonomous Vehicles, and Same-Day Shipping 45
13- The Impact of Big Data: Leveraging Customer Insights for Growth 49
14- E-Commerce Marketplaces: The Power of Collaboration 53
15- The Future of Online Payments: Cryptocurrencies and Beyond 57

Conclusion 61

ACKNOWLEDGMENTS

I might want to offer my most profound thanks and appreciation to every one of the people who have added to the production of this book. Without their help, support, and direction, this venture could never have been conceivable.

I, first and foremost, might want to thank my family for their enduring affection and understanding all through the creative cycle. Their understanding, support, and faith in me have been a steady wellspring of inspiration.

I'm hugely appreciative to my supervisor, whose aptitude and sharp eye have enormously worked on the nature of this book. Their clever criticism, fastidious altering, and significant ideas have helped shape this work into its last structure.

I might likewise want to stretch out my genuine thanks to my exploration colleagues and beta readers, who devoted their time and work to give significant experiences and criticism. Their feedback has been instrumental in refining the thoughts and ideas introduced in this book.

I'm obligated to my coaches and instructors who have directed and propelled me along my composing process. Their insight, information, and faithful help have been priceless in molding my comprehension and supporting my development as an essayist.

An extraordinary thank you goes to my companions and partners who offered their support and shouted out to me during the ups and downs of this innovative flow. Your expressions of help and excitement have kept me still up in the air to own this venture.

I might want to offer my thanks to the distributing group, cover architects, and everybody engaged with the development of this book. Your impressive skill, devotion, and obligation to greatness have guaranteed that this work arrives at its readers in the most ideal manner.

In conclusion, I need to stretch out my most profound appreciation to the readers. Your advantage in this book and your eagerness to leave on this excursion with me is genuinely lowering. It is my sincerest expectation that the words inside these pages impact you, motivate you, and give you pleasure.

Much obliged to you for being a piece of this undertaking. Your help and confidence in me have meant everything, and I'm always appreciative.

With genuine appreciation,

[Shahid Gill].

Beyond the Checkout

Exploring the Future of Online Shopping

Introduction

Welcome to "Beyond the Checkout: Exploring the Future of Online Shopping." In this eBook, we embark on a journey to uncover the exciting possibilities that lie ahead in the world of e-commerce. The rapid advancement of technology, changing consumer behaviors, and the ever-expanding digital landscape are reshaping the way we shop and interact with retailers online.

Gone are the days when online shopping merely involved browsing through product listings, adding items to a virtual cart, and proceeding to checkout. The future of online shopping holds promises of personalized experiences, immersive virtual environments, voice-activated purchases, and seamless integration across various channels.

In this digital age, retailers and consumers alike are constantly adapting to new trends and innovations. The purpose of this eBook is to shed light on the emerging technologies, trends, and strategies that will shape the future of online shopping. We will explore the cutting-edge advancements that are revolutionizing the e-commerce industry and examine how they will impact businesses and consumers.

Throughout the chapters that follow, we will dive into topics such as augmented reality (AR) and virtual reality (VR) shopping experiences, the rise of voice commerce powered by intelligent assistants, the integration of artificial intelligence

(AI) in e-commerce, and the influence of mobile commerce (M-commerce) in shaping the future of online shopping. We will also explore the intersection of social media and e-commerce, the role of blockchain in ensuring secure transactions, the growing importance of sustainability and ethical shopping, and the impact of big data on understanding customer preferences and behavior.

Moreover, we will discuss the concept of Omni channel retailing, which blurs the boundaries between physical and online stores, and examine the future of delivery logistics, including the utilization of drones, autonomous vehicles, and same-day shipping services. Additionally, we will delve into the growing significance of e-commerce marketplaces, the potential of cryptocurrencies as a means of online payment, and the overall implications of these developments on the future of online shopping.

By gaining insights into these areas, we hope to equip businesses and consumers with the knowledge and understanding necessary to navigate the evolving landscape of e-commerce. Whether you are an entrepreneur looking to thrive in the digital marketplace or a shopper seeking to make the most of your online experience, this eBook will provide you with valuable insights and foresight into the future of online shopping.

So, let us embark on this journey together and discover what lies beyond the checkout. The future of online shopping awaits us, and the possibilities are limitless.

1- The Rise of Online Shopping: A Brief History

The world of online shopping has arisen a long way since its beginning. In this chapter, we will take a step back in time to explore the roots and evolution of online shopping. By understanding the historical context, we can appreciate the transformative journey that has led us to the present state of e-commerce.

1.1 The Birth of E-Commerce:

The early beginnings: The emergence of online transactions and electronic commerce.

Pioneering technologies: The development of secure protocols and encryption for online transactions.

The first online retailers: Examining the early players who paved the way for online shopping.

1.2 The Dot-Com Boom:

The internet revolution: The widespread adoption of the Internet and its impact on commerce.

The rise of e-commerce startups: The birth of iconic online retailers and their strategies.

Challenges and lessons: Exploring the successes and failures during the dot-com era.

1.3 The E-Commerce Giants:

The Establishment of Amazon: Jeff Bezos' Vision and the Growth of the online retail behemoth.

The rise of eBay: The transformation of online auctions into a global marketplace.

Other influential players: Alibaba, Walmart, and the global expansion of e-commerce.

1.4 Changing Consumer Behavior:

Internet penetration and digital literacy: The factors driving the adoption of online shopping.

The impact of convenience: How e-commerce revolutionized the way we shop.

Shifting consumer expectations: From price comparisons to personalized experiences.

1.5 E-Commerce Technologies:

Advancements in payment systems: The evolution of online payment methods.

Logistics and fulfillment: Innovations in supply chain management and delivery services.

The role of data analytics: Harnessing customer insights to improve the online shopping experience.

1.6 Regulatory and Legal Considerations:

Consumer protection and online security: Balancing convenience with privacy and safety.

International regulations: Navigating cross-border transactions and legal frameworks.

1.7 The Impact of Mobile Devices:

The rise of smartphones: How mobile technology reshaped online shopping.

Mobile apps and mobile commerce: Expanding opportunities and convenience for consumers.

1.8 The Pandemic Acceleration:

COVID-19 and its impact: How the global pandemic accelerated the growth of online shopping.

Changing consumer habits: The shift from brick-and-mortar stores to online platforms.

The rise of online shopping has been a remarkable journey, marked by technological advancements, changing consumer behaviors, and global events. In this chapter, we have explored the historical timeline of e-commerce, from its early beginnings to the current state of the industry. Understanding this history is crucial to grasp the transformative power of online shopping and anticipating the future trends that will shape the e-commerce landscape.

2- Current State of Online Shopping: Trends and Statistics

In this chapter, we will explore the current state of online shopping, examining the latest trends, consumer behaviors, and key statistics that define the e-commerce landscape. By understanding the present landscape, businesses can make informed decisions and adapt their strategies to meet the evolving demands of online shoppers.

2.1 E-Commerce Market Size:

Global e-commerce market: An overview of the current size and growth trajectory.

Regional variations: Examining the e-commerce markets in different regions and their growth patterns.

Market segments: Analyzing the growth of different product categories in online retail.

2.2 Mobile Commerce (M-Commerce):

The rise of mobile shopping: Statistics on the increasing use of smartphones and tablets for online shopping.

Mobile app usage: The impact of mobile apps on consumer engagement and purchase behavior.

Mobile payment trends: The adoption of mobile payment systems and their influence on m-commerce.

2.3 Cross-Border E-Commerce:

Globalization of online shopping: The growth of cross-border e-commerce and its impact.

Popular cross-border marketplaces: Examining the platforms that facilitate international online transactions.

Consumer preferences in cross-border shopping: Factors influencing cross-border purchasing decisions.

2.4 Personalization and Customization:

Tailoring the online experience: The importance of personalized recommendations and targeted marketing.

User-generated content: The role of reviews, ratings, and social proof in online purchase decisions.

Customization options: The demand for personalized products and services in online retail.

2.5 Omnichannel Retailing:

Seamless integration: The merging of online and offline channels for a unified shopping experience.

Click-and-collect: The growth of in-store pickups for online orders.

Showrooming and web rooming: Consumer behaviors that bridge the gap between online and offline shopping.

2.6 Social Commerce:

Social media as a shopping platform: The impact of social networks on e-commerce.

Influencer marketing: Leveraging social media influencers to drive product discovery and sales.

Shop able content: The integration of e-commerce features into social media platforms.

2.7 Sustainability and Ethical Shopping:

The rise of conscious consumerism: The growing demand for eco-friendly and socially responsible products.

Ethical considerations: Consumer attitudes towards fair trade, supply chain transparency, and sustainability.

Sustainable packaging and shipping: Innovations in eco-friendly packaging and delivery practices.

2.8 Emerging Technologies in Online Shopping:

Artificial Intelligence (AI): How AI is transforming online shopping through personalized experiences and chatbots.

Augmented Reality (AR) and Virtual Reality (VR): The use of immersive technologies for enhanced product visualization.

Voice Commerce: The rise of voice-activated shopping through virtual assistants.

Conclusion:

The current state of online shopping is dynamic and ever-evolving, driven by changing consumer behaviors and technological advancements. In this chapter, we have explored the latest trends and key statistics that define the e-commerce landscape. By understanding these trends, businesses can stay ahead of the curve and adapt their strategies to meet the evolving demands and expectations of online shoppers.

3- The Power of Personalization: Tailoring the Shopping Experience

In today's competitive e-commerce landscape, personalization has emerged as a powerful tool for businesses to enhance the shopping experience and drive customer engagement. In this chapter, we will delve into the concept of personalization and its significance in online shopping. We will explore how businesses can leverage personalization strategies to create tailored experiences that resonate with individual customers.

3.1 Understanding Personalization:

Defining personalization: Exploring the different aspects and levels of personalization in e-commerce.

The value of personalization: Examining the benefits and advantages of implementing personalized strategies.

3.2 Collecting Customer Data:

Data-driven personalization: The role of customer data in creating personalized experiences.

Types of customer data: Exploring demographic, behavioral, and preference data for personalization.

Ethical considerations: Balancing data collection with privacy and security concerns.

3.3 Personalized Product Recommendations:

Recommendation algorithms: The use of machine learning and AI to generate personalized product suggestions.

Collaborative filtering: Leveraging user behavior and preferences to offer relevant recommendations.

Dynamic and real-time recommendations: Tailoring suggestions based on current browsing and purchase behavior.

3.4 Personalized Email Marketing:

Segmentation and targeting: Dividing customers into specific segments for personalized email campaigns.

Behavioral triggers: Sending automated emails based on customer actions and preferences.

Customized content and offers: Tailoring email content to match individual interests and needs.

3.5 Website Personalization:

Dynamic content: Displaying customized content and product recommendations based on user behavior.

Personalized landing pages: Tailoring landing pages to match specific customer segments or campaigns.

User interfaces and experiences: Adapting website elements to provide a personalized and intuitive journey.

3.6 Personalized Customer Service:

Chatbots and virtual assistants: Using AI-powered tools to provide personalized customer support.

Omnichannel customer service: Seamlessly integrating customer interactions across various channels.

Proactive customer engagement: Anticipating customer needs and reaching out with personalized assistance.

3.7 Personalization Challenges and Best Practices:

Data privacy and security: Ensuring customer trust while collecting and utilizing personal data.

Scaling personalization efforts: Overcoming challenges in implementing personalization on a larger scale.

Continuous optimization: Iterative testing and refinement to improve the effectiveness of personalization strategies.

Personalization has become a key differentiator in the competitive online shopping landscape. In this chapter, we have explored the power of personalization and its ability to create tailored shopping experiences. By collecting and leveraging customer data, businesses can deliver personalized product recommendations, email marketing campaigns, website experiences, and customer service interactions. However, it is crucial to navigate the challenges of data privacy and security while implementing personalization strategies. By continuously optimizing and refining personalization efforts, businesses can build strong customer relationships, increase engagement, and drive conversions in the ever-evolving world of e-commerce.

4- Augmented Reality (AR) and Virtual Reality (VR): Transforming the Shopping Experience

Augmented Reality (AR) and Virtual Reality (VR) technologies have revolutionized the way customers interact with products and brands in the online shopping space. In this chapter, we will explore the transformative impact of AR and VR on the shopping experience. We will delve into their applications, benefits, and prospects in e-commerce.

4.1 Understanding Augmented Reality (AR) and Virtual Reality (VR):

Differentiating AR and VR: Exploring the fundamental concepts and technologies behind AR and VR.

Immersive experiences: Understanding how AR and VR create realistic and interactive virtual environments.

Hardware and software requirements: Examining the devices and platforms used for AR and VR experiences.

4.2 Augmented Reality (AR) in Online Shopping:

Product visualization: Enhancing the customer's ability to visualize products in their environment.

Virtual try-on: Allowing customers to virtually try on clothing, accessories, and cosmetics.

Home and interior design: Enabling customers to visualize furniture, decor, and renovations in their space.

4.3 Virtual Reality (VR) in Online Shopping:

Virtual stores and showrooms: Replicating the in-store experience in a virtual environment.

Immersive product demonstrations: Providing customers with interactive and detailed product experiences.

Virtual events and experiences: Host virtual product launches, fashion shows, and exclusive events.

4.4 Benefits and Advantages of AR and VR in Online Shopping:

Enhanced customer engagement: Increasing customer interaction and involvement with products.

Reduced product returns: Allowing customers to make informed purchase decisions through realistic previews.

Brand differentiation: Setting brands apart by offering cutting-edge and memorable shopping experiences.

4.5 Overcoming Challenges and Adoption Barriers:

Technological limitations: Addressing hardware requirements and compatibility issues.

User experience considerations: Designing intuitive and user-friendly AR and VR interfaces.

Cost and scalability: Balancing the investment required with the potential returns on AR and VR implementation.

4.6 Case Studies: Successful Implementations of AR and VR in E-commerce:

Fashion and beauty industry: Showcasing how AR and VR have transformed the try-on experience.

Furniture and home decor: Demonstrating how AR and VR enable customers to visualize products in their space.

Automotive and electronics: Highlighting how AR and VR enhance product exploration and customization.

4.7 Future Trends and Possibilities:

Advancements in AR and VR technology: Exploring emerging innovations and their impact on online shopping.

Social and collaborative experiences: Leveraging AR and VR to enable shared shopping experiences.

Integration with other technologies: Examining the synergy between AR, VR, AI, and voice commerce.

Augmented Reality (AR) and Virtual Reality (VR) have opened up new horizons for online shopping, transforming the way customers interact with products and brands. In this chapter, we have explored the applications, benefits, and challenges of AR and VR in e-commerce. As these technologies continue to advance and become more accessible, businesses that embrace AR and VR have the opportunity to provide immersive, engaging, and personalized shopping experiences. By staying at the forefront of AR and VR developments, businesses can differentiate themselves, captivate customers, and shape the future of online shopping.

5- Voice Commerce: From Voice Assistants to Voice-Activated Shopping

Voice commerce, powered by voice assistants and natural language processing, has emerged as a disruptive force in the world of online shopping. In this chapter, we will explore the evolution of voice commerce and its impact on the shopping experience. We will delve into the capabilities of voice assistants, voice-activated shopping, and the opportunities and challenges that businesses face in this voice-driven landscape.

5.1 The Rise of Voice Assistants:

Introduction to voice assistants: Understanding the technology behind popular voice assistants.

Adoption and usage trends: Examining the increasing popularity and usage of voice assistants.

Voice assistant ecosystems: Exploring the integration of voice assistants into various devices and platforms.

5.2 Voice Search and Product Discovery:

The shift to voice search: Analyzing the growing reliance on voice search for product information.

Optimizing for voice search: Strategies to enhance product visibility and discoverability in voice searches.

Conversational commerce: Understanding how voice assistants provide personalized product recommendations.

5.3 Voice-Activated Shopping:

Voice-controlled transactions: Enabling customers to make purchases through voice commands.

Seamless reordering: Simplifying the repurchasing process through voice-activated reordering.

Voice payments: Exploring the integration of voice assistants with secure and convenient payment systems.

5.4 Enhancing the Shopping Experience with Voice:

Personalized shopping experiences: Leveraging voice assistants to offer tailored product suggestions.

Voice-guided navigation: Assisting customers in navigating through product catalogs and online stores.

Product information and reviews: Providing detailed product descriptions and user reviews through voice interactions.

5.5 Challenges and Considerations in Voice Commerce:

Voice recognition accuracy: Addressing challenges related to voice accuracy and understanding.

Privacy and security: Ensuring the protection of customer data and secure voice transactions.

Multilingual and multicultural support: Catering to diverse customer demographics and language preferences.

5.6 Voice Commerce in Different Industries:

Retail and e-commerce: Examining how voice commerce impacts online shopping experiences.

Travel and hospitality: Exploring the integration of voice assistants in travel bookings and hotel reservations.

Food and grocery delivery: Leveraging voice commerce for seamless ordering and delivery services.

5.7 Future Trends and Innovations:

Advanced natural language processing: Enhancing voice assistants' understanding and conversational capabilities.

Voice commerce in smart home ecosystems: Exploring voice-enabled smart home devices and their impact on shopping.

Integration with other technologies: Voice commerce's synergy with AI, IoT, and personalized marketing.

Voice commerce has transformed the way customers interact with brands and make purchases in the online shopping landscape. In this chapter, we have explored the rise of voice assistants, the role of voice search and product discovery, and the potential of voice-activated shopping. While there are challenges to overcome, businesses that embrace voice commerce have the opportunity to provide convenient, personalized, and frictionless shopping experiences. By staying ahead of voice commerce trends and adopting innovative strategies, businesses can capture the attention and loyalty of customers in this voice-driven era of online shopping.

6- Artificial Intelligence (AI) in E-Commerce: Enhancing Recommendations and Customer Service

Artificial Intelligence (AI) has revolutionized the e-commerce industry by enabling businesses to deliver personalized recommendations and exceptional customer service. In this chapter, we will explore the various applications of AI in e-commerce, focusing on how it enhances product recommendations and customer support. We will delve into the underlying technologies, benefits, and challenges associated with AI implementation in the e-commerce space.

6.1 Understanding Artificial Intelligence (AI) in E-Commerce:

Defining AI and its relevance in the e-commerce industry.

Machine learning and deep learning: Core technologies powering AI-driven solutions.

Importance of data: Leveraging large-scale data for AI algorithms and models.

6.2 Personalized Product Recommendations:

Recommendation engines: How AI-powered algorithms generate personalized product suggestions.

Collaborative filtering: Leveraging user behavior and preferences to enhance recommendations.

Content-based filtering: Analyzing product attributes and descriptions to offer relevant recommendations.

6.3 AI Chatbots and Virtual Assistants:

Chatbot automation: How AI-driven chatbots handle customer inquiries and provide support.

Natural Language Processing (NLP): Understanding and interpreting customer queries.

Conversational AI: Enabling dynamic and human-like interactions with customers.

6.4 AI-Powered Customer Service:

Sentiment analysis: Utilizing AI to gauge customer sentiment and provide appropriate responses.

Customer support automation: AI-driven solutions for issue resolution and troubleshooting.

Proactive customer engagement: AI's ability to predict customer needs and offer tailored assistance.

6.5 Fraud Detection and Risk Management:

AI in fraud prevention: Detecting fraudulent transactions and mitigating risks.

Pattern recognition: Identifying suspicious activities and anomalies in real-time.

Adaptive security measures: Leveraging AI to strengthen data protection and security.

6.6 Benefits and Advantages of AI in E-Commerce:

Personalized shopping practices: Enhancing purchaser satisfaction and visit.

Increased conversions and sales: AI's ability to recommend relevant products and boost purchase decisions.

Improved operational efficiency: Automating tasks and streamlining customer service processes.

6.7 Ethical and Privacy Considerations:

Data privacy and security: Safeguarding customer information and ensuring compliance.

Transparency and accountability: Establishing ethical AI practices and responsible data usage.

Balancing personalization and privacy: Striking the right balance between customization and customer consent.

6.8 Case Studies: Successful AI Implementations in E-Commerce:

Amazon's recommendation engine: Examining how AI drives personalized product recommendations.

Virtual assistants in customer service: Showcasing how AI-powered chatbots improve support experiences.

Fraud detection in financial services: Demonstrating the effectiveness of AI in mitigating risks.

6.9 Future Trends and Innovations:

Predictive analytics: AI's role in forecasting customer behavior and anticipating market trends.

Visual search: AI-driven solutions that enable customers to search for products using images.

Hyper-personalization: Advancements in AI to deliver even more tailored and individualized experiences.

Artificial Intelligence (AI) has become a game-changer in the e-commerce industry, elevating the customer experience through personalized product recommendations and improved customer service. In this chapter, we explored the various applications of AI, including recommendation engines, AI chatbots, and virtual assistants. By harnessing the power of AI, businesses can enhance customer satisfaction, drive conversions, and streamline operations. However, it is essential to address ethical considerations and ensure the privacy and security of customer data. As AI continues to evolve, businesses that embrace innovative AI-driven strategies will gain a competitive edge in the dynamic e-commerce landscape.

7- Mobile Commerce (M-Commerce): The Future in the Palm of Your Hand

Mobile commerce (M-commerce) has transformed the way consumers shop and interact with brands, offering convenience, accessibility, and personalized experiences. In this chapter, we will explore the rise of M-commerce and its implications for businesses. We will delve into the unique features and opportunities that mobile devices present, as well as the challenges and best practices for successful M-commerce implementation.

7.1 The Mobile Revolution:

Evolution of mobile devices: From feature phones to smartphones and their impact on commerce.

Mobile Internet penetration: Analyzing the widespread adoption and usage of mobile Internet.

Shifting consumer behaviors: Understanding how mobile devices have changed shopping habits.

7.2 Mobile Shopping Apps:

The rise of shopping apps: Exploring the popularity and benefits of dedicated mobile shopping applications.

Features and functionalities: Examining key features such as product search, personalized recommendations, and easy checkout.

Optimizing app performance: Strategies for improving app speed, responsiveness, and user experience.

7.3 Mobile-Optimized Websites:

Responsive design: Creating websites that adapt to different mobile screen sizes and resolutions.

Streamlined checkout process: Simplifying the mobile purchasing journey to minimize friction.

Performance optimization: Enhancing website speed and load times for optimal mobile browsing.

7.4 Mobile Payments:

Mobile wallet solutions: Exploring popular mobile payment platforms and their integration with M-commerce.

One-click payments: Enabling convenient and secure checkout experiences on mobile devices.

NFC and contactless payments: Leveraging near-field communication technology for seamless transactions.

7.5 Location-Based Services and Personalization:

Geolocation technology: Utilizing location data to offer personalized recommendations and promotions.

Local inventory availability: Informing customers about nearby stores and product availability.

Targeted push notifications: Sending relevant and timely notifications to engage mobile users.

7.6 Mobile Advertising and Marketing:

In-app advertising: Targeting users with relevant ads within mobile applications.

Mobile search ads: Optimizing ad campaigns for mobile search engine results in pages.

SMS and push notifications: Leveraging direct messaging channels for promotional offers and updates.

7.7 Mobile Customer Support:

Mobile-friendly customer service channels: Providing chat and messaging support optimized for mobile devices.

In-app help and tutorials: Assisting customers with self-service options within mobile applications.

Social media engagement: Utilizing mobile platforms for real-time customer interactions and issue resolution.

7.8 Security and Trust in M-Commerce:

Mobile security considerations: Protecting customer data and securing mobile transactions.

Building trust: Implementing robust security measures and transparent data handling practices.

User authentication: Balancing convenience and security with biometric authentication and two-factor authentication.

7.9 Future Trends in M-Commerce:

Mobile voice search: Exploring the integration of voice assistants and voice-activated shopping on mobile devices.

Augmented Reality (AR) in M-commerce: Enhancing the mobile shopping experience through AR overlays.

Mobile commerce in emerging markets: Understanding the unique opportunities and challenges in developing regions.

Mobile commerce (M-commerce) has become an integral part of the e-commerce landscape, offering businesses unparalleled opportunities to engage with customers on a personal and convenient level. In this chapter, we explored the various aspects of M-commerce, including mobile apps, mobile-optimized websites, mobile payments, and location-based services. By embracing M-commerce and implementing mobile-centric strategies, businesses can cater to the growing mobile consumer base, drive sales, and build long-lasting customer relationships. As technology continues to advance, businesses must stay agile and adapt to emerging trends in M-commerce, ensuring they stay at the forefront of the ever-evolving mobile landscape.

8- Social Commerce: The Intersection of Social Media and Online Shopping

Social commerce has emerged as a powerful trend in the e-commerce industry, blurring the lines between social media and online shopping. In this chapter, we will explore the concept of social commerce and its impact on businesses and consumers. We will delve into the integration of social media platforms with e-commerce, the rise of influencer marketing, and the strategies for successful social commerce implementation.

8.1 Understanding Social Commerce:

Defining social commerce and its evolution in the digital landscape.

Social media platforms as e-commerce channels: Exploring the convergence of social media and online shopping.

The role of user-generated content: Harnessing customer-generated content for social commerce.

8.2 Social Media Platforms as Shopping Destinations:

Instagram Shopping: Leveraging visual content and shoppable posts on Instagram.

Facebook Marketplace: Creating a peer-to-peer selling platform within Facebook.

Pinterest Shopping: Utilizing visual discovery and product pins for shopping experiences.

8.3 Influencer Marketing and Brand Collaborations:

The power of influencers: Understanding the impact of influencer marketing on consumer behavior.

Identifying the right influencers: Strategies for finding influencers who align with your brand.

Collaborating with influencers: Building partnerships and leveraging influencer reach for social commerce.

8.4 Social Commerce Features and Tools:

Shop able posts: Enabling direct product links and purchase options within social media content.

Social shopping carts: Allowing users to add products to a cart and make purchases without leaving the platform.

Social reviews and recommendations: Harnessing social proof and user-generated content for product discovery.

8.5 Social Commerce Analytics and Insights:

Monitoring social commerce performance: Measuring engagement, conversions, and customer behavior.

Leveraging social listening: Utilizing social media data to identify trends and customer preferences.

Iterative optimization: Using analytics to refine social commerce strategies and enhance performance.

8.6 Building Trust and Engagement in Social Commerce:

Transparency and authenticity: Fostering trust through transparent communication and genuine interactions.

User-generated content and social proof: Encouraging customers to share their experiences and reviews.

Community-building: Creating a sense of belonging and engagement through social media communities.

8.7 Social Commerce Advertising:

Targeted social media ads: Utilizing advanced targeting options to reach relevant audiences.

Retargeting and remarketing: Engaging potential customers who have shown interest in your products.

Native advertising: Integrating branded content seamlessly into users' social media feeds.

8.8 Social Commerce and Customer Service:

Social media as a customer support channel: Providing real-time assistance and issue resolution.

Social listening for customer feedback: Monitoring social media conversations to address customer concerns.

Turning customers into brand advocates: Encouraging satisfied customers to share their experiences on social media.

8.9 Ethical Considerations and Challenges in Social Commerce:

Transparency and disclosure: Ensuring clear disclosure of sponsored content and partnerships.

Privacy and data protection: Safeguarding customer data in social commerce interactions.

Maintaining authenticity: Balancing promotional content with genuine interactions and community-building.

Social commerce has revolutionized the way consumers discover and purchase products, leveraging the power of social media platforms and influencer marketing. In this chapter, we explored the concept of social commerce, the integration of social media platforms with e-commerce, and the strategies for successful implementation. By embracing social commerce and building meaningful connections with customers on social media, businesses can tap into a vast audience, drive engagement, and increase sales. As social media continues to evolve, businesses must stay agile and adapt their social commerce strategies to leverage emerging trends and technologies.

9- The Role of Blockchain in E-Commerce: Security and Transparency

Blockchain technology has emerged as a disruptive force in various industries, including e-commerce. In this chapter, we will explore the role of blockchain in e-commerce and its potential to enhance security and transparency in online transactions. We will delve into the fundamental concepts of blockchain, its benefits for e-commerce businesses, and the challenges and considerations in its implementation.

9.1 Understanding Blockchain Technology:

Introduction to blockchain: Explaining the decentralized and distributed ledger technology.

Blockchain components: Understanding blocks, transactions, and consensus mechanisms.

Smart contracts: Exploring self-executing contracts and their applications in e-commerce.

9.2 Enhancing Security in E-Commerce with Blockchain:

Data encryption and immutability: Leveraging blockchain's cryptographic features to secure transaction data.

Fraud prevention: Prevent unauthorized access, identity theft, and tampering with e-commerce data.

Supply chain transparency: Verifying product authenticity and tracking the movement of goods through blockchain.

9.3 Building Trust and Transparency:

Immutable transaction records: Ensuring transparency and audibility of e-commerce transactions.

Customer reviews and ratings: Creating trustworthy feedback systems using blockchain-based reputation management.

Counterfeit prevention: Using blockchain to verify the authenticity of products and reduce counterfeiting.

9.4 Streamlining Payments and Transactions:

Peer-to-peer transactions: Facilitating direct transactions between buyers and sellers without intermediaries.

Cross-border transactions: Simplifying international payments and reducing transaction costs with blockchain.

Faster settlements and reduced fees: Enhancing the efficiency of payment processing in e-commerce.

9.5 Loyalty Programs and Tokenization:

Blockchain-based loyalty programs: Improving customer loyalty and engagement through tokenized rewards.

Token economies: Exploring the use of blockchain tokens as a medium of exchange within e-commerce ecosystems.

Tokenized assets and ownership: Enabling fractional ownership and transferability of digital assets.

9.6 Challenges and Considerations in Blockchain Adoption:

Scalability and performance: Addressing the limitations of blockchain in handling high-volume e-commerce transactions.

User experience: Ensuring a seamless and user-friendly blockchain experience for e-commerce customers.

Regulatory compliance: Navigating legal and regulatory frameworks surrounding blockchain and e-commerce.

9.7 Case Studies: Successful Blockchain Implementations in E-Commerce:

Supply chain management: Examining how blockchain improves traceability and transparency in supply chains.

Payment solutions: Showcasing blockchain-based payment platforms and their impact on e-commerce.

Digital identity management: Leveraging blockchain for secure and decentralized identity verification in e-commerce.

9.8 Future Trends and Innovations:

Interoperability between blockchain networks: Enabling seamless integration and data exchange across different blockchains.

Integration with Internet of Things (IoT): Exploring the synergy between blockchain and IoT devices in e-commerce.

Decentralized marketplaces: Examining the potential of blockchain-powered peer-to-peer marketplaces.

Blockchain technology offers e-commerce businesses a promising solution to enhance security, transparency, and efficiency in online transactions. In this chapter, we explored the role of blockchain in e-commerce, from improving security measures to streamlining payments and building trust among participants. While blockchain adoption in e-commerce presents challenges, the potential benefits make it an exciting technology for businesses to explore. By embracing blockchain and its applications, e-commerce companies can foster a secure and transparent environment, thereby building trust with customers, reducing fraud, and unlocking new opportunities for innovation. As blockchain continues to evolve, businesses that stay abreast of emerging trends and leverage its capabilities will be well-positioned to thrive in the rapidly evolving e-commerce landscape.

10- Sustainability and Ethical Shopping: Navigating the Green Consumer Revolution

The rise of sustainability and ethical concerns has transformed consumer behavior, prompting a shift towards conscious shopping practices. In this chapter, we will explore the importance of sustainability and ethics in e-commerce and how businesses can navigate the green consumer revolution. We will delve into sustainable sourcing, eco-friendly packaging, responsible manufacturing, and the strategies for implementing ethical practices in the e-commerce industry.

10.1 The Rise of Green Consumerism:

Understanding the motivations behind sustainable and ethical consumer behavior.

The impact of environmental and social awareness on e-commerce.

The role of certifications and labeling in ethical shopping.

10.2 Sustainable Sourcing and Supply Chains:

Responsible sourcing practices: Promoting fair labor, environmental stewardship, and social responsibility.

Supporting local communities: Fostering partnerships with local artisans and producers.

Traceability and transparency: Ensuring visibility into the supply chain and verifying sustainable sourcing claims.

10.3 Eco-Friendly Packaging:

Sustainable packaging materials: Exploring alternatives to traditional packaging materials, such as biodegradable or recycled options.

Minimizing waste: Adopting minimalist packaging designs and reducing excessive packaging.

Packaging optimization: Streamlining packaging processes to reduce carbon footprint and transportation costs.

10.4 Responsible Manufacturing:

Ethical labor practices: Ensuring fair wages, safe working conditions, and labor rights for workers.

Carbon-neutral manufacturing: Implementing energy-efficient practices and offsetting carbon emissions.

Product lifecycle management: Encouraging repair, recycling, and responsible disposal of products.

10.5 Green Marketing and Consumer Education:

Communicating sustainability efforts: Transparently sharing information about sustainable practices with consumers.

Educating consumers: Raising awareness about the environmental and social impact of consumer choices.

Green messaging and branding: Aligning brand values with sustainability to attract conscious consumers.

10.6 Partnerships with Sustainability Initiatives:

Collaboration with non-profit organizations: Supporting environmental and social causes through strategic partnerships.

Offset programs and carbon neutrality: Participating in initiatives to offset carbon emissions and promote environmental conservation.

Circular economy initiatives: Exploring partnerships that enable the recycling and repurposing of products and materials.

10.7 Consumer Engagement and Empowerment:

Providing sustainability information: Offering detailed product information, including sourcing, manufacturing, and environmental impact.

Customer involvement in sustainability initiatives: Encouraging consumers to participate in recycling programs or donate to environmental causes.

Feedback and transparency: Welcoming consumer feedback and openly addressing concerns regarding sustainability practices.

10.8 Measuring and Reporting Sustainability:

Key performance indicators (KPIs) for sustainability: Identifying metrics to assess and track environmental and social impact.

Sustainability reporting: Communicating progress and achievements through sustainability reports.

Third-party certifications and audits: Seeking independent validation of sustainable practices.

10.9 Ethical Challenges and Considerations:

Greenwashing: Avoiding misleading or deceptive sustainability claims.

Balancing affordability and sustainability: Offering sustainable options at accessible price points.

Addressing global supply chain complexities: Navigating ethical challenges in a globalized marketplace.

The green consumer revolution has ushered in a new era of sustainability and ethical shopping in the e-commerce industry. In this chapter, we explored the importance of sustainability and ethics, from responsible sourcing and eco-friendly packaging to responsible manufacturing and consumer education. By embracing sustainability and ethical practices, e-commerce businesses can align with the values of conscious consumers, differentiate themselves in the market, and contribute to a more sustainable future. As the demand for sustainable and ethical products continues to grow, businesses that prioritize sustainability and navigate the associated challenges will be well-positioned to thrive in the evolving consumer landscape while making a positive impact on the environment and society.

11- Omni-Channel Retailing: Seamlessly Integrating Offline and Online Shopping

In today's interconnected world, consumers expect a seamless shopping experience that bridges the gap between online and offline channels. Omni-channel retailing has emerged as a strategy to integrate these channels and provide a unified customer experience. In this chapter, we will explore the concept of omnichannel retailing, its benefits for businesses and consumers, and the strategies for successfully implementing an omnichannel approach.

11.1 Understanding Omni-Channel Retailing:

Definition and evolution of omnichannel retailing.

The importance of channel integration in meeting customer expectations.

Key components of a successful omnichannel strategy.

11.2 Creating a Consistent Brand Experience:

Brand identity across channels: Ensuring a consistent brand image and messaging.

Seamless design and user experience: Providing a cohesive and intuitive experience across online and offline touchpoints.

Integrated loyalty programs: Reward customers for engagement and purchases across channels.

11.3 Integrated Inventory and Fulfillment:

Real-time inventory visibility: Enabling customers to check product availability across all channels.

Buy online, pick up in-store (BOPIS): Allowing customers to purchase online and collect their orders from a physical store.

Ship-from-store: Utilizing store inventory to fulfill online orders and reduce delivery times.

11.4 Unified Customer Profiles and Data Integration:

Single customer view: Consolidating customer data from various channels to create a holistic view.

Personalization and targeted marketing: Leveraging customer insights to deliver tailored experiences and offers.

Cross-channel tracking and attribution: Understanding customer behavior and attributing sales to the appropriate channels.

11.5 Seamless Customer Journey:

Channel continuity: Allowing customers to switch channels seamlessly without losing their progress or information.

Consistent pricing and promotions: Ensuring that pricing and promotional offers are aligned across channels.

Integrated customer service: Providing consistent support and assistance regardless of the channel.

11.6 Leveraging Technology and Tools:

Point-of-sale (POS) integration: Connecting online and offline sales systems for centralized data management.

Mobile apps and in-store technology: Enhancing the in-store experience with mobile apps, interactive displays, and self-checkout options.

Cross-channel analytics: Analyzing data from multiple channels to gain insights and optimize strategies.

11.7 Omni-Channel Marketing and Communication:

Integrated marketing campaigns: Creating cohesive marketing messages and promotions across channels.

Channel-specific targeting: Tailoring marketing efforts to each channel's audience and characteristics.

Cross-channel communication: Ensuring seamless communication between online and offline channels.

11.8 Training and Empowering Staff:

Cross-channel training: Equipping employees with the knowledge and skills to deliver a seamless customer experience.

Empowering in-store associates: Enabling staff to access customer information and assist with online purchases in-store.

Aligning incentives: Rewarding employees for delivering exceptional Omni-channel experiences.

11.9 Measuring Success and Iterative Improvement:

Key performance indicators (KPIs) for Omni-channel retailing: Identifying metrics to assess the effectiveness of channel integration.

Customer feedback and satisfaction: Gather insights from customers to understand their experience and make necessary improvements.

Continuous optimization: Iteratively refining Omni-channel strategies based on data and customer feedback.

Omni-channel retailing has become a necessity for businesses seeking to meet the evolving expectations of customers who desire a seamless shopping experience. In this chapter, we explored the concept of Omni-channel retailing, from creating a consistent brand experience to integrating inventory, data, and customer profiles. By implementing a successful Omni-channel strategy, businesses can enhance customer satisfaction, improve brand loyalty, and drive sales across multiple channels. As technology continues to advance and customer preferences evolve, businesses must stay agile and continuously adapt their Omni-channel approach to deliver the best possible customer experience. By embracing Omni-channel retailing, businesses can position themselves at the forefront of the retail industry and create a competitive advantage in a digitally-driven marketplace.

12- The Future of Delivery: Drone, Autonomous Vehicles, and Same-Day Shipping

The landscape of product delivery is rapidly evolving, driven by advancements in technology and changing consumer expectations. In this chapter, we will explore the future of delivery, focusing on the emerging trends of drone delivery, autonomous vehicles, and same-day shipping. We will delve into the potential benefits and challenges associated with these innovations, as well as their impact on the e-commerce industry and customer experience.

12.1 Drone Delivery:

Introduction to drone technology: Exploring the capabilities and potential of unmanned aerial vehicles (UAVs) in delivery.

Advantages of drone delivery: Discuss the speed, efficiency, and accessibility benefits offered by drones.

Regulatory considerations: Examining the legal and regulatory framework surrounding drone delivery operations.

12.2 Autonomous Vehicles:

Self-driving vehicles in delivery: Understanding the use of autonomous cars, trucks, and robots for last-mile delivery.

Safety and reliability: Addressing concerns and advancements in autonomous vehicle technology.

Infrastructure requirements: Exploring the infrastructure needed to support the widespread adoption of autonomous delivery vehicles.

12.3 Same-Day Shipping:

Consumer expectations: Analyzing the rise in demand for faster delivery options.

Operational challenges: Discuss the logistical complexities of implementing same-day shipping.

Strategies for efficient same-day shipping: Exploring warehouse optimization, route planning, and real-time tracking.

12.4 Last-Mile Innovations:

Micro-fulfillment centers: Examining the concept of localized fulfillment centers for faster delivery.

Locker systems and pickup points: Exploring alternative delivery methods that offer convenience and flexibility to customers.

Crowd shipping and peer-to-peer delivery: Leveraging the sharing economy to facilitate localized delivery services.

12.5 Sustainability and Environmental Considerations:

Green delivery solutions: Assessing the environmental impact of various delivery methods and exploring eco-friendly alternatives.

Electric and alternative fuel vehicles: Examining the potential for reducing carbon emissions in delivery operations.

Optimization and consolidation: Discuss strategies to minimize delivery miles and enhance operational efficiency.

12.6 Data Analytics and Optimization:

Route optimization algorithms: Utilizing data analytics and machine learning to optimize delivery routes and improve efficiency.

Predictive analytics: Forecasting demand patterns to optimize inventory management and delivery operations.

Real-time tracking and customer communication: Enhancing visibility and providing proactive updates to customers.

12.7 Customer Experience and Expectations:

Convenience and speed: Meeting customer demands for quick and hassle-free delivery experiences.

Flexibility and control: Providing options for delivery time windows, rerouting, and alternative delivery locations.

Personalization and customization: Tailoring delivery experiences based on customer preferences.

12.8 Security and Privacy:

Addressing concerns related to data privacy and security in delivery operations.

Preventing theft and ensuring the secure handling of packages during transit.

Implementing secure authentication and verification processes.

12.9 Future Challenges and Considerations:

Public acceptance and adoption: Overcoming potential resistance and concerns from the public regarding new delivery technologies.

Infrastructure development: Investing in the necessary infrastructure to support advanced delivery systems.

Collaboration and regulatory frameworks: Establishing partnerships and regulatory frameworks to ensure safe and efficient delivery operations.

The future of delivery holds immense potential for transforming the way products reach consumers. In this chapter, we explored the emerging trends of drone delivery, autonomous vehicles, and same-day shipping, highlighting their benefits, challenges, and implications for the e-commerce industry. By embracing these innovations, businesses can enhance delivery speed, convenience, and customer satisfaction. However, the successful implementation of advanced delivery methods requires addressing regulatory, safety, and infrastructure considerations. As technology continues to advance and consumer expectations evolve, staying at the forefront of delivery innovation will be crucial for businesses to thrive in the competitive e-commerce landscape.

13- The Impact of Big Data: Leveraging Customer Insights for Growth

In the digital age, businesses have access to vast amounts of data generated by customers. Big data analytics has emerged as a powerful tool for extracting valuable insights and driving growth. In this chapter, we will explore the impact of big data on the e-commerce industry and how businesses can leverage customer insights to fuel growth and enhance the customer experience.

13.1 Understanding Big Data in E-commerce:

Definition and characteristics of big data.

Sources of big data in e-commerce: website analytics, transactional data, customer interactions, social media, etc.

Challenges and opportunities associated with big data analytics.

13.2 Customer Segmentation and Targeting:

Behavioral segmentation: Analyzing customer behavior to identify distinct segments and their preferences.

Personalization strategies: Tailoring marketing messages, product recommendations, and offers to specific customer segments.

Predictive analytics: Using historical data to predict customer behavior and target them with relevant marketing efforts.

13.3 Enhanced Customer Experience:

Improving website usability and user experience based on data insights.

Optimizing product recommendations and cross-selling opportunities.

Proactive customer service: Utilizing data to anticipate customer needs and provide personalized support.

13.4 Pricing and Promotion Optimization:

Dynamic pricing: Leveraging real-time data to adjust prices based on demand, competition, and customer behavior.

Promotional strategies: Analyzing the effectiveness of promotions and optimizing promotional campaigns based on customer response.

A/B testing: Conducting controlled experiments to determine the most effective pricing and promotional strategies.

13.5 Supply Chain Optimization:

Demand forecasting: Using data analytics to forecast customer demand and optimize inventory management.

Inventory optimization: Analyzing data to determine optimal stocking levels and minimize stock-outs.

Supplier management: Utilizing data insights to identify reliable suppliers and optimize supply chain processes.

13.6 Fraud Detection and Risk Management:

Fraud detection algorithms: Analyzing patterns and anomalies in data to identify fraudulent activities.

Risk assessment and mitigation: Utilizing data to assess and mitigate potential risks in e-commerce operations.

Cybersecurity: Employing data-driven approaches to protect customer data and prevent data breaches.

13.7 Marketing Attribution and ROI Analysis:

Determining the impact of marketing campaigns and attributing sales to specific marketing channels.

Return on investment (ROI) analysis: Measuring the effectiveness of marketing efforts based on data-driven insights.

Optimizing marketing spending: Allocating resources to the most profitable marketing channels based on data analysis.

13.8 Competitive Intelligence:

Market analysis: Analyzing market trends, competitor strategies, and customer sentiment to gain a competitive edge.

Pricing intelligence: Monitoring competitors' pricing strategies and adjusting pricing accordingly.

Product development and innovation: Leveraging data insights to identify gaps in the market and develop innovative products.

13.9 Ethical Considerations and Data Privacy:

Ensuring submission with data shield regulations and safeguarding purchaser privacy.

Transparency and consent: Communicating data collection and usage practices to customers.

Responsible data usage: Using data ethically and responsibly, respecting customer preferences and rights.

Big data analytics has revolutionized the e-commerce industry by providing businesses with valuable customer insights that can drive growth and enhance the customer experience. In this chapter, we explored the impact of big data, from customer segmentation and targeting to supply chain optimization and marketing attribution. By harnessing the power of big data, businesses can make informed decisions, personalize experiences, optimize operations, and gain a competitive advantage. However, it is crucial to prioritize data privacy, ethical considerations, and transparency to build trust with customers. As technology continues to advance and data volumes increase, the effective use of big data will become even more critical for businesses to thrive in the dynamic e-commerce landscape.

14- E-Commerce Marketplaces: The Power of Collaboration

E-commerce marketplaces have revolutionized the way businesses and consumers interact in the digital era. These platforms provide a space for sellers to showcase their products and reach a broader customer base while offering consumers a wide range of choices. In this chapter, we will explore the power of collaboration through e-commerce marketplaces and how businesses can leverage these platforms to drive growth, expand their reach, and enhance the customer experience.

14.1 Understanding E-Commerce Marketplaces:

Definition and characteristics of e-commerce marketplaces.

Types of marketplaces: Generalist vs. specialist marketplaces, B2C vs. B2B marketplaces.

Benefits and challenges of selling on e-commerce marketplaces.

14.2 Expanding Reach and Customer Acquisition:

Access to a larger customer base: Tapping into the existing user base of the marketplace.

Geographic expansion: Selling to customers in new regions and countries through global marketplaces.

Targeted customer acquisition: Leveraging marketplace tools and advertising options to reach specific customer segments.

14.3 Streamlined Operations and Logistics:

Simplified product listing and management: Using marketplace tools to efficiently manage product catalog and inventory.

Order fulfillment and shipping: Leveraging marketplace logistics services or integrating with third-party logistics providers.

Customer service and returns: Utilizing marketplace infrastructure for customer support and handling returns.

14.4 Brand Exposure and Trust:

Brand visibility: Showcasing products on a trusted platform with high traffic and brand recognition.

Social proof and reviews: Leveraging customer reviews and ratings to build trust and credibility.

Marketplace branding options: Customizing storefronts and utilizing marketplace advertising features to enhance brand presence.

14.5 Competitive Insights and Pricing Strategies:

Competitive analysis: Monitoring competitor pricing, product assortment, and promotions on the marketplace.

Dynamic pricing: Adjusting prices based on real-time market data and competitor pricing intelligence.

Bundling and cross-selling opportunities: Identifying complementary products to offer bundled deals and increase average order value.

14.6 Customer Data and Personalization:

Customer insights: Leveraging marketplace data and analytics to understand customer preferences and behavior.

Personalized recommendations: Using customer data to provide tailored product recommendations and enhance the shopping experience.

Retargeting and remarketing: Reaching out to potential customers who have shown interest in your products on the marketplace.

14.7 Collaborative Partnerships and Cross-Selling:

Partnering with complementary sellers: Creating synergies by collaborating with sellers offering related or complementary products.

Cross-selling opportunities: Exploring cross-selling strategies with other sellers on the marketplace to expand customer reach.

Joint marketing efforts: Collaborating on promotional campaigns and sharing marketing resources to drive mutual growth.

14.8 International Expansion and Market Testing:

Testing new markets: Using marketplaces as a low-risk entry point to test the demand for products in new regions.

Localization and language support: Leveraging marketplace infrastructure to reach customers in different languages and cultures.

Overcoming trade barriers: Utilizing marketplace logistics and fulfillment services to overcome international shipping challenges.

14.9 Building Direct Relationships with Customers:

Customer data ownership: Balancing the benefits of marketplace reach with the importance of building direct customer relationships.

Customer retention strategies: Using marketplace sales as a stepping stone to establish direct customer relationships and repeat business.

Omnichannel integration: Integrating marketplace sales with your website or physical stores to provide a seamless customer experience.

E-commerce marketplaces provide a powerful platform for collaboration, enabling businesses to expand their reach, enhance brand exposure, and access a larger customer base. In this chapter, we explored the benefits of selling on e-commerce marketplaces, including streamlined operations, competitive insights, and opportunities for collaboration. By strategically leveraging e-commerce marketplaces, businesses can drive growth, gain market insights, and build strong customer relationships. However, it is essential to carefully manage the balance between marketplace sales and direct customer relationships to maintain control over customer data and foster long-term business sustainability. Collaborating with e-commerce marketplaces can be a key strategy for businesses to thrive in the dynamic and competitive e-commerce landscape.

15- The Future of Online Payments: Cryptocurrencies and Beyond

The world of online payments is experiencing significant transformation, focused by technological progressions and altering shopper preferences. In this chapter, we will explore the future of online payments, with a particular focus on cryptocurrencies and other emerging payment technologies. We will examine the potential benefits, challenges, and implications of these innovations for the e-commerce industry and the broader digital economy.

15.1 Evolution of Online Payments:

Overview of traditional online payment methods, such as credit cards, digital wallets, and bank transfers.

Limitations and pain points of traditional payment systems.

Need for innovation in online payments to address security, speed, cost, and inclusivity concerns.

15.2 Cryptocurrencies and Blockchain Technology:

Introduction to cryptocurrencies and blockchain technology.

The advantages of cryptocurrencies for online payments include security, transparency, and decentralization.

Major cryptocurrencies in use today, such as Bitcoin, Ethereum, and Ripple.

15.3 Cryptocurrency Adoption and Integration:

Growing acceptance of cryptocurrencies by merchants and e-commerce platforms.

Integrating cryptocurrencies as a payment option on e-commerce websites.

Overcoming challenges related to volatility, regulatory compliance, and user experience.

15.4 Decentralized Finance (DeFi) and Smart Contracts:

Exploring the potential of decentralized finance (DeFi) in revolutionizing online payments.

Smart contracts and their role in automating payment processes and reducing transaction costs.

Decentralized payment platforms and their impact on traditional financial intermediaries.

15.5 Stablecoins: Stability and Mainstream Adoption:

Understanding stablecoins and their role in mitigating the volatility of cryptocurrencies.

Different types of stablecoins, such as fiat-collateralized, crypto-collateralized, and algorithmic stablecoins.

Use cases and potential benefits of stablecoins in e-commerce transactions.

15.6 Biometric and Tokenized Payments:

Biometric authentication in online payments, such as fingerprint, facial recognition, and voice recognition.

Tokenization of payment data for enhanced security and privacy.

Advantages and challenges of biometric and tokenized payment methods.

15.7 Central Bank Digital Currencies (CBDCs):

Exploring the concept of central bank digital currencies and their potential impact on online payments.

Advantages of CBDCs, including efficiency, security, and financial inclusion.

Challenges and considerations in implementing CBDCs at a national or global scale.

15.8 Cross-Border Payments and Remittances:

Innovations in cross-border payment solutions, including blockchain-based remittance services.

Reducing costs and improving efficiency in international transactions.

Regulatory and compliance considerations in cross-border payments.

15.9 Payment Security and Fraud Prevention:

Enhancing payment security through technologies like encryption, tokenization, and multi-factor authentication.

Leveraging artificial intelligence and machine learning for fraud detection and prevention.

Protecting customer data and privacy in online payment transactions.

15.10 The Future of Online Payments:

Predictions and trends for the future of online payments.

Integration of online payments with emerging technologies, such as the Internet of Things (IoT) and artificial intelligence.

The role of collaboration between industry stakeholders in shaping the future of online payments.

The future of online payments is poised for significant innovation and disruption. In this chapter, we explored the potential of cryptocurrencies, blockchain technology, decentralized finance, stablecoins, biometric payments, central bank digital currencies, and other emerging payment technologies. These advancements have the potential to enhance security, speed, cost-effectiveness, and inclusivity in online transactions. However, there are challenges to overcome, including regulatory considerations, user adoption, and integration with existing payment infrastructure. By staying abreast of these developments and embracing the opportunities they present, businesses can position themselves at the forefront of the evolving online payments landscape.

Conclusion

In "Beyond the Checkout: Exploring the Future of Online Shopping," we have delved into the exciting realm of e-commerce and explored the possibilities that lie ahead. The journey has taken us through the evolution of online shopping, the current trends shaping the industry, and the transformative technologies that will redefine the way we shop in the future.

From personalized shopping experiences to augmented reality and virtual reality, from voice commerce to artificial intelligence, and from mobile commerce to social commerce, we have witnessed the immense potential of these advancements to enhance the online shopping journey. The integration of blockchain for secure transactions, the growing emphasis on sustainability and ethical shopping, and the power of big data in understanding consumer behavior have also been key areas of exploration.

Furthermore, we have discussed the concept of omnichannel retailing, where the lines between physical and online stores blur, and the future of delivery logistics, including the utilization of innovative methods such as drones and autonomous vehicles. We have also examined the role of e-commerce marketplaces and the potential of cryptocurrencies as a means of online payment.

As we conclude this eBook, it is evident that the future of online shopping is dynamic and ever-evolving. The possibilities are vast, and the potential for growth and innovation is immense. Businesses and consumers must adapt to these changes, embrace emerging technologies, and stay informed about the latest trends to thrive in this digital landscape.

For businesses, understanding and harnessing these advancements will enable them to create personalized, seamless, and immersive shopping experiences that resonate with their customers. By leveraging AI, utilizing innovative technologies, and leveraging data-driven insights, businesses can cultivate customer loyalty, drive sales, and stay ahead of the competition.

For consumers, the future of online shopping promises convenience, customization, and unparalleled experiences. It empowers individuals to make informed decisions, connects with brands on a deeper level, and access a global marketplace with just a few clicks.

However, as we embark on this exciting future, it is essential to keep in mind the importance of balancing innovation with ethical considerations. As technology advances, it is crucial to prioritize privacy, security, and sustainability to ensure a responsible and inclusive digital ecosystem.

In conclusion, the future of online shopping is filled with endless opportunities and transformative potential. By embracing the advancements and strategies discussed in this eBook, businesses and consumers can navigate this ever-changing landscape and unlock the full potential of e-commerce. So, let us embrace the future beyond checkout and embark on this journey together, where the world of online shopping continues to evolve and reshape our lives.